Tiny

essentials of
fundraising

White Lion
Press

I would like to thank Jodie Brownlee,
James Sloggie, Frances Sloggie,
Ken Burnett, Marie Burnett,
Jane Fricker and Ernest Muller
for their great help with
this book.

Neil

Tiny
essentials of
fundraising

by Neil Sloggie

Published by
The White Lion Press Limited
Kermarquer
56310 Melrand
France

© 2002 Neil Sloggie/The White Lion Press Limited
ISBN 0-9518971-5-2

First printed 2002
Second printing 2002
Third printing 2006
Fourth printing 2006

British Library Cataloguing – in – Publication Data.
A catalogue record for this book is available from the
British Library.

Model: Rachel Kempster

Photography by Adrian Taylor

Design and print production by *em* associates

Printed and bound in the United Kingdom by
Bell & Bain Ltd

Contents

The author

Neil Sloggie's fundraising career spans 15 years. During this time Neil has worked with a wide range of organisations in Europe, Asia, North and South America, and in Australia and New Zealand. He has made use of all fundraising techniques. Posts Neil has held have included Asia Pacific Region Fundraising Manager for Greenpeace International, Fundraising Manager for a London-based cancer charity, and senior consultant in a UK-based fundraising consultancy.

Neil is now a fundraising consultant based in Australia. He works in Australia and internationally with a range of clients.

Neil Sloggie
Telephone: +61 (0)4 1304 7905
Fax: +61 (0)7 3105 7313
Email: neil@fundraisingsolutions.com.au
www.fundraisingsolutions.com.au

Preface

There are a few fundamental strengths that are common to most successful fundraising programmes. Also, there are some mistakes that we all routinely make, no matter how long we've been in the profession. In a friendly way, this book records the principles underlying a good fundraising programme and highlights where some are likely to go wrong.

The principles have been learned through, sometimes bitter, experience and from the teachings of many very wise people.

About the 'Tiny Essentials' series

The book you hold in your hands is part of a series of little books with a big mission. They focus on what really matters in a key area of voluntary sector management. Each book's purpose is to provide the essentials of its subject in an entertaining, easily digestible form, so readers can effortlessly and enjoyably get access to what they really need to know.

'Tiny' books are delightfully free of padding, waffle and over-blown theories. Extraneous material has been reduced to a minimum; there's just no room for anything other than the essence of what really matters in the subject and how to order your priorities.

Other books in the Tiny series include:

Tiny Essentials of Writing for Fundraising, by George Smith.

Tiny Essentials of Major Gift Fundraising, by Neil Sloggie.

Tiny Essentials of an Effective Volunteer Board, by Ken Burnett

Tiny Essentials of Raising Money from Foundations and Trusts, by Jo Habib

Tiny Essentials of Monthly Committed Giving, by Harvey McKinnon

All can be ordered at www.whitelionpress.com

A **new** recruit

Kate considered her choices. She wanted to find out what made an excellent fundraiser. After several years working for a corporation she had decided to look for a job where she could really help society. Kate wanted to work for a charity or other not-for-profit organisation, to help to raise money that would be put to good use.

She knew charities took fundraising very seriously. The not-for-profit sector had grown rapidly. Large amounts were at stake; fundraisers were experienced, trained professionals. She wanted to learn as much as she could about what makes a fundraiser successful, before starting in her new career.

Kate had heard that fundraising was not a highly competitive profession – fundraisers were usually pleased to share their experience. Meeting with some successful fundraisers seemed to her a good way to learn.

She narrowed her list to three fundraising managers. Each had a very different approach and each seemed very successful. She made appointments to see all of them.

George

The first person Kate visited was George, the fundraising manager at the Healthy Improved Clean Environment Society, known as HICES. This society had a large busy fundraising department. She had heard that they concentrated mainly on asking people for donations via direct mail. A database had been built up containing records of 200,000 donors. These donors gave one-off donations which the fundraisers attempted to renew each year. The annual income was $5 million.

George was extremely busy and only able to spare a few minutes.

Kate asked what he did on an average day.

George laughed, 'In fundraising there is never an average day. Fundraising is a world in which you can never predict what will happen next. Take this morning for example. We have spent eight weeks designing an emergency appeal to go out to our donors. We want it to be as successful as our appeal last year, which won an award from the local marketing association.' George pointed proudly at an impressive looking framed certificate on the wall. 'We also wanted everyone who works here to be happy with the appeal because it is going to so many people, so we asked for comments from all staff members. We redesigned the mailing pack several times to take into account all the comments we received. Finally, agreement was reached on the text four weeks late – and it has ended up much longer than we intended.'

He continued, 'Then the appeal was delayed again when the database crashed last week. This morning I've heard we have a breakdown at the printers. We have to get the mail out in the next four days or it will get mixed up with Christmas post and lower our response. I have to deal with all these issues personally. It's an exciting job, Kate, but it can be incredibly stressful.'

Kate was silent for a short time. It did indeed seem like a very stressful, almost frantic job.

George was called away to deal with an urgent telephone call and Kate used the time alone to read the text of the emergency appeal. It seemed to her very technical and, frankly, rather boring. There was a lot about HICES but not so much about the environment, the cause that they worked on. She realised she couldn't quite remember what HICES stood for, yet it had been used frequently throughout the text.

She also reflected that George's only reference to a previous appeal was to mention he had won an award. Kate wondered if that was the way charities judged the success of their fundraising. He hadn't mentioned if it had raised much money.

As George returned, Kate was wondering why he had needed to deal with the crashed database personally, there seemed to be a lot of staff around, although they all seemed pretty busy as well.

George sat down again, looking rather distracted. The phone conversation had been about the printing. It seemed the problem at the printer was because of the volume of the mailing. The printing company was new to HICES and didn't normally deal in mailings of this size.

'But,' he explained, 'they are cheap and going with this printer did save quite a lot of money, which you must always be thinking about when you work for a charity.'

'Why do you have to send out so many letters?' Kate asked.

'We get a response rate from appeals of 10 per cent, our average gift is $30, so to make our target of $600,000, we need to send out to our whole file of 200,000 people.'

George was called away again. There was a donor in the charity's reception area asking why he hadn't received any acknowledgement of a donation sent six months ago. He was concerned that perhaps his gift had never been received.

Kate thought more carefully about George's approach to the mailing. She noted that he was concerned what the organisation's staff thought of the mailing pack, but he didn't seem to have considered what the donors might have been interested in. All staff had been involved in the writing of the letter, but he had never asked a donor to comment.

It also seemed strange to Kate that the only answer to raising $600,000 was to send the same pack to every supporter. She thought that perhaps if he researched the people on his database he might discover which part of his charity's work different groups of people were most interested in, which types of letter they responded to, or how much they tended to give. Then perhaps he could design different letters for different groups. In fact when she thought about it the list of possible ways to segment the database was very long indeed. Presumably, the more you thought about the donor and personalised the approach, the more likely they were to respond to you.

When George returned Kate asked about this.

'Kate you must understand that we have very limited resources here' he replied. 'It is far cheaper to send out the same letter to everyone.'

'Would some donors respond better to a phone call than a letter?'

George shook his head, 'No, telemarketing is far too expensive. Mail is cheaper, so better!'

'How much did the appeal cost?'

George thought for a while. 'Well, I'm not sure exactly what each appeal costs, but the overall fundraising operation returns about $2 for every $1 invested – the sort of figures commercial operators would die for! Our most significant cost is in retaining so many donors on our file, but this is also our big source of income so there's no way round it. Only 50 per cent of donors contribute each year. This means that we have to find 100,000 new ones annually, mainly through advertising and cold direct mail. Also, maintaining the database is a major expense.'

George leaped across the room and chased after a colleague he had just seen through the door. 'I need to talk with him urgently Kate, back in a moment.'

Kate looked out the window and collected her thoughts. One issue that troubled her was that George seemed to be taking a rather narrow view of the programme. He was trying to keep costs to a minimum, which seemed admirable because he was working for a charity. But was that really cost-efficient? Overall, $2 return for every $1 invested certainly seemed a fair commercial return, but looked at another way, 50 cents of each donor's dollar going on fundraising costs seemed very high.

She wondered if he had really considered that if he invested in more research and targeting in his mailing programme, the extra income might have made it worthwhile. Had he considered that the higher expense of telemarketing might increase income to such an extent that it would more than offset the increased cost?

It would be a problem, she thought, to ask a charity to increase its spending on fundraising when the cost ratio already seemed high. But perhaps it wasn't really increased expenditure that was needed at all!

Maybe George's programme just needed more focusing of fundraising spending on areas that would bring the highest return on investment.

And, losing 50 per cent of donors each year? That seemed high, was he trying as hard to keep existing donors as he was trying to get new ones?

George was back and he was getting impatient, he was running out of time. Kate decided to move on to her next question.

'Do you have any people or organisations who give you large amounts of money?'

'Yes we do have some major donors' replied George. 'We have about 10 major corporate donors who give about $50,000 when we talk them into it, several grant-giving charitable foundations who have given similar amounts and 10 extremely wealthy people who have given us donations of over $100,000 in the past. In fact, I'm sorry I haven't been able to spend more time working with our major donors. Once this appeal is out of the way I'll be devoting a substantial proportion of my time to them.'

'When was the last time you spoke with one of the major donors?' Kate asked.

'Well now I'm not sure' said George. 'I'm afraid that recently we have had one big job after another and major donors have fallen by the wayside a bit. I always have very good intentions for regular communications with them, but their needs are never as urgent as the larger group of smaller donors, so they really don't get so much attention.'

Kate left the office of HICES pleased that she had been given some time and information from such an experienced fundraiser. The meeting, though, had raised more questions with her than it had answered. She looked forward to her next meeting with Jon from the Deaf Society. Then, she was sure, it would all become clear.

Jon

Kate had heard a little about Jon from the Deaf Society already. He was also an extremely busy manager, running a large fundraising department. His, however, was focused far more on raising money from special events and from a merchandise operation, which sold goods to supporters to make a profit for the charity. He too had a database of 200,000 supporters, but his charity's annual income was $8 million. This was $3 million more than George's. The total cost of fundraising was unknown, but estimated at about 30 per cent of the income.

When she was shown into the Deaf Society's fundraising office she immediately noticed great activity. Staff moved quickly, if a little anxiously, amongst an extraordinary clutter of goods. Boxes, catalogues and greeting cards were piled to the roof.

From behind a stack of boxes of T-shirts appeared a smiling, slightly harassed looking man. 'Hello Kate, I'm Jon, what would you like to know about fundraising?'

Before Kate had a chance to start on her questions, Jon explained the intense activity surrounding them.

'A catalogue of goods for sale was posted two months ago to our 200,000 supporters. At the moment all hands are working flat out to take orders, send out goods requested, deal with returns, mistakes, complaints, wrong sizes and postal delays. The Deaf Society puts a 100 per cent mark-up on all goods for sale so it is really very profitable.'

'How about when all costs of staff time, mailing, printing and fulfillment are taken into account?' Kate asked.

'Ultimately we get about 15 per cent of the sale price going to the charity.'

Behind the room they were standing in, Kate saw many more boxes. 'That's the stock room' Jon told her. 'We forecast roughly what we will sell each year and buy it in advance. We are always left with piles of unsold stock, the size of these piles is testament to how well we forecast.'

Kate asked if any people who might otherwise make a straight donation to the charity would think that their purchase of merchandise represented their gift for the year. 'I hope not' replied Jon. 'If someone gives $100 as a straight donation we get the lot, if they buy merchandise, we see maybe $15!'

'Are special events a good source of income for you?' Kate asked.

'Let me tell you about the May Ball.' Jon was excited about this topic. 'Five hundred people attended, it was held in a five-star hotel. Tickets were $150 each. Ticket sales, a raffle and various other initiatives on the night resulted in a gross income of over $100,000 for the charity.'

'A success?' asked Kate.

'Sure,' replied Jon, 'a few celebrities even turned up.' He mentioned several names. 'It was a lot of fun on the night. I love charity balls.' Then he laughed as he recalled the panic leading up to the event. 'With only three weeks to go, not nearly enough

tickets had been sold and, because of
the major up-front guarantee required
by the hotel, we risked making a
substantial loss. This would have
caused serious cutbacks in the
charity's work. Everyone in the
Society was enlisted to help that time.
They were great. They simply
dropped everything, went out selling
tickets to everybody they knew and
within the two weeks we had sold
enough.'

Kate asked about the overall cost of
fundraising. Jon replied that it
depended how one looked at it and
what factors were taken into
consideration, what was regarded as
costs and what was considered
investment.

It all certainly seemed very
complicated.

Kate left the meeting rather worried,
with several more outstanding
questions:

If, once all costs were considered, only
15 per cent of income from the
merchandise catalogue was profit, was
it not better just to make an additional
thoughtful targeted ask to donors for
further straight donations to the

charity's work, where a far higher percentage would go to the charity?

Secondly, wouldn't the leftover stock, when written off, reduce the income of the merchandise programme still further? If they didn't forecast correctly they could even make a loss.

Why did Jon concentrate on the gross income and seem not to know the net income from the special event? Surely this was the whole point of carrying it out?

Kate wondered what had happened to the deaf people relying on the charity's services during the fundraising ball panic when all staff had had to stop work to help, presumably these services had had to stop also. And was the cost of all this extra staff time taken into account when calculating the net income, if indeed the net income was calculated at all?

And, wouldn't people give more freely and feel better about it if they were giving directly to the charity's work with deaf people rather than purchasing goods from a catalogue?

Kate had heard of many very successful fundraising events and fundraising merchandising operations.

She was sure they could make money for some organisations. But she was equally sure they needed to have more focus and more strategic consideration than Jon seemed to be applying.

The
first
essential

Kate's third meeting with a fundraising manager started completely differently. Jane from Environment and Nature Group met her at the charity's reception. She was relaxed and confident and took Kate not to the fundraising department, but to a room with a large map. She explained that the purpose of the charity was to purchase large tracts of land in environmentally sensitive areas. These could then be conserved in their natural condition, free forever from the threat of development. She pointed to an impressive number of brightly coloured green spots on the map. 'This is our progress so far,' she said, 'and these yellow areas are the ones we are targeting to buy next.'

Kate commented that the other fundraisers she had visited had really made only passing mention of their charity's actual work. 'That,' said Jane, 'is fundamental lesson number one about fundraising. People who donate most regularly and give the highest amounts are usually those who, either naturally, or because you have persuaded them, care deeply about the cause. A successful fundraiser must always keep this in mind as the reason people give. Charity fundraising that is not reaching its full potential can often be shown to have lost sight of this and to be concentrating too heavily on promoting the organisation, the staff, or some fundraising product that is not clearly related to the cause. The first essential principle is simple: always concentrate fundraising on the work of your organisation.

'Here is an example' she continued. 'Our Environment and Nature Group might try fundraising by selling watches with our name on them. Instead of telling our donors we want them to give money to save environmentally sensitive areas, we are telling them to buy this excellent watch and some of the money will go to helping our cause, which, by the way, is saving wilderness areas. You see the difference? You shift the focus from your excellent work, to the watch. They may buy it, and you get your small percentage, but when you want to persuade them to give again, you may have to offer them another product they need.

'Your results are more likely to be successful if you can persuade a group of people that it is essential for them to contribute urgently and regularly to your cause. You can provide regular updates about the good work you are doing with their money. This will make them far more likely to continue giving than the watch ever could.

'Whenever you think about your work,' Jane explained, 'or if you are describing it to friends or potential donors (everyone is a potential donor), don't think "I am a professional fundraiser and last week I had a two per cent response to a mail drop". Think and say, "*I raise funds for the Environment and Nature Group which last year saved*

100,000 hectares of beautiful untouched land from industrial development and pollution". Feels better doesn't it?

'Concentrating your fundraising on the work of the charity sounds simple but the charity world is full of distractions. Every fundraising manager receives regular suggestions about great and crazy fundraising schemes, products, events, etc. The ones that will usually work best are focused squarely on your work.'

Jane continued, 'Another example is the charity that decides to do a fiftieth anniversary appeal. Do you think people are more likely to give $100 if you write to them about the charity being 50 years old, or if you send them something saying, *"your gift of $100 will help this child who is in desperate need"*?'

Kate noted down that the first essential is

Always focus fundraising on the work of the organisation.

The
second
essential

I
**Always focus
fundraising on the
work of the
organisation.**

Jane took her to the fundraising office. Kate was amazed to find a quiet atmosphere, very different from the previous offices she had visited. Jane explained that she had five staff, a database of 200,000 donors, a gross income of $25,000,000 and fundraising costs of $5,000,000.

Kate was staggered. 'This number of donors matches those of the other fundraisers I've visited, but the income is far higher. And you are telling me exactly the fundraising cost. The others didn't mention it and when asked didn't clearly know.'

'It's not hard' replied Jane. 'It's simply commonsense and having the will to stick to that first principle, and the other six which I'll explain if you can spare the time.' Kate told her how interested she was to learn and asked her to go on and explain the further principles.

'Essential principle number two' said Jane, 'is to concentrate your effort on the areas of your programme that produce the best return on investment. Simple isn't it? But again it's a principle from which many fundraisers are easily distracted.

'A minority of donors will give the majority of the income and from a fundraising point of view they deserve the most attention. But it is the big majority of smaller donors that demand by far the most attention and that's where the distraction lies. The top five per cent of your donors will give substantial amounts and will be the least demanding, but from your income point of view they deserve the most attention of all. I reserve one day each week simply for phone calls and visits to major donors. I have a list of 100 that I deal with personally, each has the capability of giving $50,000. Ignoring them because I'm too busy organising an event that would net $40,000 wouldn't be sensible would it? Also, I have a major gift fundraiser who deals personally and solely with the next 1,000 highest donors.'

'This seems straightforward' said Kate. Then she remembered the Deaf Society Ball and mentioned it to Jane.

'Charity balls and special events can work really well' Jane commented. 'However you need a very good fundraising reason to justify running one. One reason is if your constituency (your target group of potential donors) is made up of people who are most likely to want to give in this way and are unlikely to give if just asked for the sake of the charity itself. If this is the case and you are an expert, with an excellent group of volunteer helpers, a special event can make good money for the charity and it can introduce new members who are in the slightly wealthier category. However they are risky, as Jon has seen. When calculating net income you must take

I
Always focus
fundraising on the
work of the
organisation.

|
Always focus
fundraising on the
work of the
organisation.

into account all expenses, including all staff time invested. Sometimes after doing these calculations you will find that they make very little money, or run at a loss. Of course you never hear about that sort of thing!'

Jane continued, 'The same principle applies to small or start-up operations, or one-off capital campaigns. If you want to raise $1 million, the first question you should ask yourself is, "*is there one source that can provide all this money?*" Then ask, "*are there two sources?*" and so on. It's not too smart to go to the expense and effort of finding 100,000 people who can give you $10 each, when one of them can give you the whole lot, is it?

'I wonder if any of the other fundraising managers you visited mentioned legacy or bequest fundraising?' Jane asked. Kate replied that they hadn't.

'This is another example of concentrating on areas of highest return,' Jane explained, 'and how easy it is to get distracted from them. There is little doubt that asking your supporters to leave money to your cause in their will is one of the most efficient types of fundraising. Many charities develop a substantial part of their income from bequests at minimal cost, but again it does not have the urgency of many other forms of fundraising. It is a simple and cost-efficient matter to remind our supporters regularly in a sensitive way that they can leave a bequest in their will to our charity. It is also quite straightforward to make sure we continue a good relationship with those who tell us they've mentioned us in their will. But because it doesn't have the urgency of a huge print run, or a stock sale of almost dated merchandise, we can often get distracted.

'It's a simple message,' Jane continued, 'concentrate your efforts on the areas of your fundraising programme which produce the best return on investment but, as you see, it is made complicated by the huge amounts of distractions all fundraising managers have to face.'

Kate thought about the people she had met previously. It was clear that they had been putting a lot of effort into getting many very small gifts, while not concentrating enough on the higher netting areas of fundraising.

She wrote down the second essential principle

I
Always focus
fundraising on the
work of the
organisation.

Concentrate your efforts on the areas of your fundraising programme which produce the best return on investment.

The
third
essential

1
Always focus
fundraising on the
work of the
organisation.

2
Concentrate your
efforts on the
areas of your
fundraising
programme which
produce the best
return on
investment.

'Jane, could you tell me more about the major gift fundraiser you mentioned earlier, who concentrates on raising money from 1,000 of the best donors?'

'That's Peter,' Jane replied, 'he's out at the moment, in fact he is out most of the time visiting donors. If he's in the office for more than about half a day at a time, I want to know why!'

Kate asked, 'Isn't this where he works?'

1
Always focus
fundraising on the
work of the
organisation.

2
Concentrate your
efforts on the
areas of your
fundraising
programme which
produce the best
return on
investment.

'Yes,' Jane laughed, 'but his job is working with people who give us larger gifts. Speaking personally face to face with a potential donor is nearly always the most effective way to secure a donation. Therefore, when people have the potential to give large amounts it is always best to invest some personal time on them. In fact this is the third essential principle of fundraising and one of the most important: people give to people.

'If a donor can afford to give $10,000,' Jane explained, 'I want to make sure that he or she gives $10,000, not $100. If Peter visits, he can invest time in really getting the message across in the way he thinks will appeal most, convincing the person of the need to give as much as he can afford and answering any questions he might have.'

'But,' said Kate, 'wouldn't it be cheaper to send a mailing?'

'Of course, but a mailing pack must to an extent be standardised to fit large numbers of people and it can't answer all the questions that might come up. Also, when people are making larger donations they often want to know personally to whom they are entrusting their money. It costs more to send Peter but, since the donations are so much larger as a result, it is an extremely worthwhile investment.'

Jane continued, 'We find personal contact is essential for corporate fundraising. If we can build relationships with the people who are responsible for giving money, we put ourselves in a far stronger position than an organisation that just writes asking for a donation. Corporations have told us in the past that there are three key reasons they turn down requests for funding.

'First they don't have a clear enough idea about exactly what the charity is asking for. Second they have some unanswered question about the charity. And third the individuals making the decision haven't built a feeling of trust in the charity.

'Through our personal relationships we can be sure of getting our request accurately at the right time to the right person, and with the best chance of success.

'With major gift, corporate, and trust fundraising we operate on the principle that we must cover for every eventuality and whatever can go wrong surely will. For example, we will always contact the

1
Always focus fundraising on the work of the organisation.

2
Concentrate your efforts on the areas of your fundraising programme which produce the best return on investment.

1
Always focus
fundraising on the
work of the
organisation.

2
Concentrate your
efforts on the
areas of your
fundraising
programme which
produce the best
return on
investment.

secretary of any committee considering giving us money on the night prior to the committee meeting. Often we find that a committee member has raised a late question, or the secretary personally has an issue that needs an answer before funds can be agreed. One simple call can eliminate this risk, but you couldn't easily place the call unless you had been building a personal relationship already with the secretary.'

'OK, I understand,' said Kate as she wrote down the third essential principle

People give to people.

'How about your smaller one-off donors, people who just give occasionally?' asked Kate.

'Actually we hardly have any donors who just give occasionally,' Jane replied, 'in fact we don't really go out looking for occasional donors. We are searching always for those who can make a long-term commitment to the charity. I think it's time we went to see Mark.'

The
fourth
essential

1
Always focus
fundraising on the
work of the
organisation.

2
Concentrate your
efforts on the
areas of your
fundraising
programme which
produce the best
return on
investment.

3
People give to
people.

Jane took Kate through the light and airy building to a large glass-fronted office. She introduced her to Mark, the Direct Marketing Manager. He said he'd been expecting her.

Mark began, 'I think Jane has taken you through the first three principles of effective fundraising, now I want to tell you the fourth, which we find is central to our programme. The fourth essential principle of fundraising is to recruit

I
Always focus
fundraising on the
work of the
organisation.

2
Concentrate your
efforts on the
areas of your
fundraising
programme which
produce the best
return on
investment.

3
People give to
people.

your supporters who give small amounts to automatic payment as soon as possible.

'By automatic payment I mean when donors sign an authority to instruct their bank or credit card company to transfer automatically an amount on a regular basis, usually monthly, from their bank account to ours.

'The charities who fundraise using a sponsor-a-child scheme learned this lesson many years ago and the rest of us are catching on slowly. We learned the hard way. People who give us one gift a year usually need us to remind them to give another, sometimes they need several reminders. About 30 per cent of these donors will end their support to us every year. We only lose 10 per cent of our donors who give by automatic payment each year and we don't have the expense of renewal and reminder letters and calls.

'With occasional donations people need to take a new decision and make an effort every time they give. With automatic payments, they have to make an effort *not* to give because they need to cancel the payment. Also, they tend to give us a higher average gift, particularly when it is monthly automatic payment.

'Some charities have a huge membership that they have to renew annually. They often have to spend enormous amounts on persuading people to give again. Eighty per cent of our donors give by monthly or annual automatic payment either by direct debit, electronic funds transfer from their bank account to ours, or from their credit card. This gives us a virtually guaranteed income from the majority of our donors. Every month the bank transfers an average of $10 from about 160,000 donors to our account. Having the income automatically transferred really beats having to ask for it each time. And it cuts costs dramatically.'

Mark went on to describe his programme, which consisted largely of looking after the committed donors. 'Our programme recruits new donors direct to auto-payment at around $10 per month using mail and advertising. We also use large-scale, face-to-face solicitation, which is where our fundraising staff and volunteers try to recruit new supporters by presenting the work of the charity during a brief conversation on the street or at a shopping centre.

'Once our donors are committed, we

I
Always focus fundraising on the work of the organisation.

2
Concentrate your efforts on the areas of your fundraising programme which produce the best return on investment.

3
People give to people.

look after them very well. We make sure
they all receive regular, interesting and
motivating communications about our
work. This is the best way to ensure
they don't stop giving. Our hope is
always that our donors will stay with us,
upgrade to a higher level of giving,
perhaps make a major gift or leave
money to the charity in their will.'

Kate thought back to the other charities
she had seen. They were spending large
amounts renewing supporters every
year, running merchandise programmes
and special events. Here it seemed so
simple. The charity worked to build up
a large number of automatic payers,
then could sit back and watch the
money roll in.

'So the majority of your income just
arrives automatically,' she asked, 'your
biggest task is the nice job of keeping
supporters up to date and ensuring they
feel good enough about your cause that
they have no desire to cancel their
automatic payment?'

'Precisely' said Mark. 'We do go into a
lot more detail with analysis of what
part of the donor life-cycle they are
most likely to quit and structure our
communications around these times,
but really the big point is the automatic
payment. It can reduce attrition

dramatically and substantially increase average gifts. Sometimes we go out looking for people who will give us single small donations, but only with the specific objective of upgrading those supporters to auto-payments. This should be the principle even if you are starting a new charity. Ten new donors giving $10 per month automatically can, over time, be worth the same as up to 200 new donors giving one-off gifts which you try to renew annually.'

Kate wrote down the fourth essential principle

Recruit your supporters to automatic payment as soon as possible.

1
Always focus
fundraising on the
work of the
organisation.

2
Concentrate your
efforts on the
areas of your
fundraising
programme which
produce the best
return on
investment.

3
People give to
people.

4
Recruit your
supporters to
automatic
payment as soon
as possible.

The
fifth
essential

Mark said, 'The fifth essential principle is to make sure you are looking after your existing donors before recruiting new ones.

'Donors are individuals' said Mark, 'and you have to treat them as such. Your ultimate goal is to tailor your programme to suit your individual donors as much as possible. This would include regular targeted asks for money, regular thanks and feedback. This is done to ensure that donors are giving to their capacity and are pleased and proud to be doing so. If you have donors who are not giving to capacity, or if you have a high rate of donors who are stopping giving, it is usually more cost-effective to concentrate on resolving this than going out looking for new donors.

'It's very straightforward and obvious really' Mark went on. 'If someone gave $10,000 last year, it is clearly better to look after him or her with a view to soliciting $15,000 or $20,000 this year, even finding ways to involve his or her contacts, rather than going completely cold to find new major donors. Likewise with smaller gifts – if you can introduce a programme of excellent communication to cut attrition on a 200,000 list from 30 per cent to 28 per cent, you just effectively recruited 4,000 new donors per year. Or if you raise the average gift on your 200,000 list from $30 to $35 you just made $1 million, equivalent to 33,000 new supporters.

'There is a time for new supporter acquisition of course and usually it happens concurrently with these measures. But some charities will forsake true effective supporter servicing for the easier to quantify new

1
Always focus fundraising on the work of the organisation.

2
Concentrate your efforts on the areas of your fundraising programme which produce the best return on investment.

3
People give to people.

4
Recruit your supporters to automatic payment as soon as possible.

1
Always focus
fundraising on the
work of the
organisation.

2
Concentrate your
efforts on the
areas of your
fundraising
programme which
produce the best
return on
investment.

3
People give to
people.

4
Recruit your
supporters to
automatic
payment as soon
as possible.

supporter acquisition and this can be a costly mistake.'

Kate thought about this. Again it seemed such commonsense, but she had seen other charities not following this logic. She wrote down the fifth essential principle

Make sure you are looking after your existing donors before recruiting new ones.

The
sixth
essential

'Essential principle number six,' Mark explained, 'is to think from the donor's point of view.

'When you compose a fundraising letter you might start by thinking, "I wonder what I want to say to the donor?" But, perhaps you would be better saying, "I wonder what the donor will be most interested in?" Or even better, "I wonder what would be

1
Always focus
fundraising on the
work of the
organisation.

2
Concentrate your
efforts on the
areas of your
fundraising
programme which
produce the best
return on
investment.

3
People give to
people.

4
Recruit your
supporters to
automatic
payment as soon
as possible.

5
Make sure you are
looking after your
existing donors
before recruiting
new ones.

most likely to persuade the donor to give?" And in all your dealings with donors it is useful to continually ask, "I wonder how the donor would most like to be treated?"

'With all donors you are trying to build a long-term partnership. You are striving together, to meet the charity's objective. Successful relationships need partners to consider each other's needs. Partnerships can fail because one partner doesn't listen, or because one partner tries to impose his or her interests or views on another.'

'Talking face to face with the donor is ideal then?' Kate asked.

'Exactly!' Mark replied. 'When you actually get to meet the potential donor you can really refine this approach. Through questioning you can sensitively deduce which type of approach is best and what area of your charity's work the potential donor is most interested in. Then using the most appropriate wordings you can show donors how much their contribution can benefit the work in the particular area.'

Kate said, 'But with the smaller donors, you can't afford to deal individually with every one. Can you really apply the same principle?'

'Yes you can' Mark said. 'In direct marketing you can do exactly the same thing, but because you are dealing with smaller donors it will usually be more cost-effective to deal with groups of people rather than individuals. Some donors will be interested in one area, some in another, there will be different times of the year when some want to give, different response rates to mail or phone, different levels of gift and so on.'

'So,' Kate summed up, 'the more you listen to your donors and the more you take that information and intelligently use it in your communications with the donor, the more successful and longer term your fundraising partnership with your donors should be.'

'Exactly' said Mark with a warm smile.

Kate thought of George and HICES and his one letter designed by the whole organisation to 200,000 people. He really wasn't designing his communications from the donors' point of view at all. It was no wonder he has such high attrition of donors,

1
Always focus fundraising on the work of the organisation.

2
Concentrate your efforts on the areas of your fundraising programme which produce the best return on investment.

3
People give to people.

4
Recruit your supporters to automatic payment as soon as possible.

5
Make sure you are looking after your existing donors before recruiting new ones.

1
Always focus
fundraising on the
work of the
organisation.

2
Concentrate your
efforts on the
areas of your
fundraising
programme which
produce the best
return on
investment.

3
People give to
people.

4
Recruit your
supporters to
automatic
payment as soon
as possible.

5
Make sure you are
looking after your
existing donors
before recruiting
new ones.

and such a big cost of fundraising.

She noted the sixth essential principle

Think from the donors' point of view.

The
seventh
essential

1
Always focus
fundraising on the
work of the
organisation.

2
Concentrate your
efforts on the
areas of your
fundraising
programme which
produce the best
return on
investment.

3
People give to
people.

4
Recruit your
supporters to
automatic
payment as soon
as possible.

5
Make sure you are
looking after your
existing donors
before recruiting
new ones.

6
Think from the
donors' point of
view.

Mark showed Kate through to the
programme department of the
charity, where they also had a big map
showing the areas of land they were
planning to buy. He joked a little with
the programme officers about the latest
land acquisition, which would make
them bigger than the local state parks
authority. Kate was surprised at how
well the fundraisers seemed to get on
with the rest of the organisation. She
had heard there was sometimes friction

I
Always focus fundraising on the work of the organisation.

2
Concentrate your efforts on the areas of your fundraising programme which produce the best return on investment.

3
People give to people.

4
Recruit your supporters to automatic payment as soon as possible.

5
Make sure you are looking after your existing donors before recruiting new ones.

6
Think from the donors' point of view.

between the department who raised the money and the one that spent it. She mentioned this to Mark.

'Don't forget principle number one about concentrating the fundraising on the work of the charity' he replied. 'In order to do this we work very closely with our land purchase and land management people. We work in planning and implementation teams with them and they spend time working in fundraising. It is essential to set good integration between departments as a priority goal. If you don't, you fall out of touch. Lack of communication causes major problems. It is very difficult to follow principle number one if you don't know what's going on.

'Also, this brings us to essential principle seven. This is the most important principle of fundraising: every fundraiser should be proud of the work they are fundraising for and be proud to ask for money for it.'

Mark continued, 'You must be proud that you are working for a charity and proud of the work that is being done. I've met some people who are a little ashamed to be working for charity. They don't see it as a fully respectable career or something. They will call themselves marketing professionals working for HICES or some other acronym. Please avoid this when you start to work with charities. You will be a fundraiser in a charity or a not-for-profit organisation that seeks to help the world in some way. And you are proud to be asking people to spend their money on that, rather than on a brand of perfume or whatever.

'And not only must the fundraisers feel this way. Ideally those who carry out the programme work of the charity should be so involved with the fundraising that they also feel good about asking for money, because they too can see how much a donation can really help.'

Kate thought about some of the reactions of her friends and relatives when she told them she was leaving her marketing career to be a fundraiser – really a second rate career, not a proper job, not a career move, a professional beggar, not really very wise. What a strange society, where some people truly think it more 'wise' or 'respectable' to be engaged in creating strategies to sell products which might be unneeded, polluting or unhealthy, than to create strategies to raise money to save lives or to campaign for a clean sustainable future.

1
Always focus fundraising on the work of the organisation.

2
Concentrate your efforts on the areas of your fundraising programme which produce the best return on investment.

3
People give to people.

4
Recruit your supporters to automatic payment as soon as possible.

5
Make sure you are looking after your existing donors before recruiting new ones.

6
Think from the donors' point of view.

She nodded slowly as she took a note of the seventh essential principle

1
Always focus fundraising on the work of the organisation.

2
Concentrate your efforts on the areas of your fundraising programme which produce the best return on investment.

3
People give to people.

4
Recruit your supporters to automatic payment as soon as possible.

5
Make sure you are looking after your existing donors before recruiting new ones.

6
Think from the donors' point of view.

Every fundraiser should be proud of the work they are fundraising for and be proud to ask for money for it.

Conclusion

1
Always focus fundraising on the work of the organisation.

2
Concentrate your efforts on the areas of your fundraising programme which produce the best return on investment.

3
People give to people.

4
Recruit your supporters to automatic payment as soon as possible.

5
Make sure you are looking after your existing donors before recruiting new ones.

6
Think from the donors' point of view.

7
Every fundraiser should be proud of the work they are fundraising for and be proud to ask for money for it.

Mark showed Kate back to an office where Jane was waiting. He left them together and Kate related some of what she had learned. She also wanted to ask a final question about the principles. 'I believe that I understand fully what I have been told and I agree with all the principles. They all seem quite simple and straightforward. I can't imagine anyone disagreeing with them. And yet before I came here I saw

1
Always focus
fundraising on the
work of the
organisation.

2
Concentrate your
efforts on the
areas of your
fundraising
programme which
produce the best
return on
investment.

3
People give to
people.

4
Recruit your
supporters to
automatic
payment as soon
as possible.

5
Make sure you are
looking after your
existing donors
before recruiting
new ones.

6
Think from the
donors' point of
view.

7
Every fundraiser
should be proud of
the work they are
fundraising for and
be proud to ask
for money for it.

examples of charities who were just not sticking to these principles at all.'

She described how the charity called HICES (she still couldn't remember what it stood for) were concentrating on one-off donations without thinking from the donors' point of view, not concentrating on the work of the charity, with no personal contact, and not focusing on higher netting areas. And the Deaf Society, which also seemed focused on high cost, low net programmes at the expense of major donors and other higher income programmes that focused on the work of the charity. Indeed their programmes may well have been actively attracting donors away from the higher income programmes. And neither of them had seemed particularly proud of what they were doing.

Jane smiled, 'We understand that situation completely, we've been through many of these problems here in the past. Actually that's why we developed these principles. Every day you will be tempted by distractions from these principles, don't succumb. Many people are attracted to fundraising because they think it will be just creative and spontaneous, they think there may not be structures or clear proven fundraising strategies and mechanisms. Some of these people can be tempted by the many wild and wacky high profile *miracle cure* type ideas that we are regularly presented with. Don't ever stifle your creativity but, equally if you are going to try new ideas, don't take your main programme too far away from these core principles.

'If you are going to be a good fundraising manager, Kate, you need above all to retain focus on your goal. When you start working with charities, if you can remember these principles and not be distracted from them, you will be clearly working within the tried and tested way of reaching that goal.'

Kate noted that Jane had said *when* you start working with charities. She assumed that she, Kate, would definitely now go to work for a charity. She mentioned it.

'Yes,' Jane laughed, 'we tend to assume that when you have seen a successful charity working you won't want to go back to the corporate sector. Usually we're right!'

1
Always focus fundraising on the work of the organisation.

2
Concentrate your efforts on the areas of your fundraising programme which produce the best return on investment.

3
People give to people.

4
Recruit your supporters to automatic payment as soon as possible.

5
Make sure you are looking after your existing donors before recruiting new ones.

6
Think from the donors' point of view.

7
Every fundraiser should be proud of the work they are fundraising for and be proud to ask for money for it.

Other books from The White Lion Press

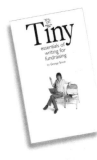

Tiny Essentials of Writing for Fundraising

by George Smith
Softback, 65 pp. ISBN 0-9518971-6-0

> 'I suggest your heart would soar if you received a letter written in decent English, which moved you and stirred your emotions, which angered you or made you proud, a letter apparently written by one individual to another. For you never see these letters any more...'

If you believe words matter then this little book is for you; it will change forever the way you communicate.

'This is a refreshing, delightfully short, guide to the author's insights about the writer's craft. If you're even thinking about writing fundraising letters you have to buy this remarkable little book.'
Mal Warwick, chairman, Mal Warwick & Associates Inc, USA.

'I am a huge fan of George's blunt but refined writing, his clear and individual voice – keep this wonderful little book next to your pen and pc.'
Lyndall Stein, CEO, Concern, UK.

'The 11,149 words in this lovely book have been carefully selected and assembled to help you write well enough to convince anyone of anything.'
Ken Burnett, author, *Relationship Fundraising*; chairman, The Cascaid Group, UK.

Tiny Essentials of Major Gift Fundraising

by Neil Sloggie
Softback, 61 pp. ISBN 0-9518971-7-9

The natural successor to Neil Sloggie's first book, *Tiny Essentials of Fundraising*, this 'Tiny' contains in their purest, most distilled form the priceless secrets of a neglected area of vast fundraising potential.

'Help is close at hand in this small gem – wise counsel, the importance of colleagues and networking, heaps of practical advice. To borrow Neil's words, "keep this one near the top of your priority pile".'
Sue-Anne Wallace, chief executive officer, Fundraising Institute-Australia.

'… a really helpful guide, especially to someone just starting out or wishing to do a quick reappraisal of their operation.'
Nick Booth, campaign director, NSPCC 'Full Stop' campaign, UK.

'… very accessible and conversational… a must for all those considering or involved in this form of fundraising.'
Maggie Taylor, consultant and trainer, UK.

Tiny Essentials of an Effective Volunteer Board

by Ken Burnett
Softback, 81 pp. ISBN 0-9518971-8-7

When Warren Maxwell is suddenly propelled into the chairman's seat of the voluntary organisation on whose board he serves, he decides that his somewhat mediocre board is going to become a paragon of all that's excellent in nonprofit governance. Join him on his quest to discover what makes a highly effective volunteer board.

'This excellent book is essential for every board member of a charity. I realise how much better a chair and trustee I could have been if only the book had been written 30 years earlier.'
Lord Joel Joffe, former chair of trustees, Oxfam UK and chair, The Giving Campaign, UK.

'This tiny book is a huge contribution to the literature on governing boards. Told as a compelling story, the insights and experience-based facts are woven skilfully throughout. A delight to read, the lessons fly off the page.'
Kay Sprinkel Grace, author, *Beyond Fundraising* and *The Ultimate Board Member's Book*, USA.

'This energising, readable book draws out what's really important, the true "tiny essentials". The 21 keys summarised in chapter six are the cream on the cake…'
Noerine Kaleeba, chair of trustees, ActionAid International, South Africa.

'This little book is absolutely brilliant; it's easy to read and is full of useful information on how to improve the effectiveness of trustee boards.

Tracy Saunders, information officer, in *Volunteering Magazine* July 2006, UK.

'In every field there are those who become the "philosophers" of their fields. Burnett is such a philosopher for the field of fundraising. He is, in essence, a "guru".

'Burnett's new book is appropriate for his status as fundraising guru since it exhibits the wisdom and in-depth thinking that is characteristic of one who is steeped in the history, philosophy, and literature of the field.'

Joanne Fritz, in a review on the website Nonproft Charitable Orgs (part of the New York Times Group) August 2006, USA.

Tiny Essentials of Raising Money from Foundations and Trusts

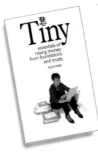

by Jo Habib
Softback, 77 pp.
ISBN 0-9518971-9-5

Of all the world's major donors (and they are major, giving away £33 billion plus each year in the UK and USA alone), foundations and trusts may be the most pure. They have no function other than to give their money away. In *Tiny Essentials of Raising Money from Foundations and Trusts*, Jo Habib shows you with precision how to get your share.

'This book brings clarity to a world that is often apparently obscure and will help anyone understand the steps that need to be taken when approaching others for money. Written clearly and simply it will be invaluable both to the novice and to experienced old hands who think they really understand their target market. It is definitely essential reading.'

Julia Unwin, consultant and author, *The Grant-Making Tango*, UK.

'This is an excellent book. Accessible and sophisticated, it is filled with smart and incisive insights on how charities can make successful inroads with foundation funders. Don't let its brevity fool you, this book is built on a deep understanding of charities,

institutional philanthropy and fundraising relationship building.'
Tim Draimin, executive director, Tides Canada Foundation, Canada.

Tiny Essentials of Monthly Committed Giving

by Harvey McKinnon
Softback, 70 pp. ISBN-13: 978-0-9553993-0-5; ISBN-10: 0-9553993-0-0

This book clearly describes the secrets of committed giving, what they are and what they require. In an entertaining, readable yet practical way the author shares his insights, experience and wisdom.

'I read this Tiny book on the bus and made heads turn by laughing out loud several times. It is easy to read, easy to understand and will be easy to use since the 43 best ideas are summed up at the end. Veteran fundraiser Harvey McKinnon even gives you the answers to convince your mule of a boss that it is time to try monthly giving, now.'
Joan Flanagan, author, *Successful Fundraising*, USA.

'Everyone has time to read a tiny book and after you read this one, you'll be able to raise lots more money for your cause through setting up a monthly donor program. This is one of the best uses of an hour that I can think of.'
Rosemary Oliver, development director, Amnesty International, Canada.

'Harvey McKinnon's latest book is a kind of bedtime story for sleepless adults – those who run financially-strapped nonprofits. If you read it tonight, you'll sleep more peacefully. Tomorrow, you'll start raising more money.'
Andy Robinson, author, *Big Gifts for Small Groups and Grassroots Grants*, USA.

'This tiny guide has given philanthropy a huge gift. McKinnon's entertaining style whilst sharing his formidable fundraising skills is in itself an act of selfless generosity.'
Lelei LeLaulu, president, Counterpart International; chairman, Foundation of the Peoples of the South Pacific, USA.

The Zen of Fundraising

by Ken Burnett
Published by Jossey-Bass Inc in
association with The White Lion
Press Limited. Softback, 169 pp.
ISBN 978-0-7879-8314-7

If all that has ever been said and
written about fundraising could be
distilled into what really matters
there would be only a small number
of true gems deserving of the
description 'nuggets of information'.

Ken Burnett has identified and defined 89 such nuggets in *The Zen of Fundraising* – a fun-to-read, one-of-a-kind look into what makes donors tick and, more importantly, what makes them give.

'Ken Burnett knows what donors want and how fundraisers can provide it. *The Zen of Fundraising* illustrates simple yet hard-earned lessons through which fundraisers can engage their donors as real partners, raising more money than ever. But to succeed, fundraisers need to aspire to greater levels of communication and donor engagement. This books shows us how.'
Chuck Longfield, founder and CEO, Target Software Inc, USA.

'The refreshingly brief principles provide inspiration and learning to anyone striving for exceptional fundraising practice.'
Nicci Dent, director of fundraising, Médecins sans Frontières, Australia.

'A gentle blend of humour, personal experiences and practical examples (but underpinned by pure steel), this book makes the most compelling case yet for thinking about donor relationships.'
Adrian Sargeant, adjunct professor of philanthropy, Indiana University Center on Philanthropy, USA.

Relationship Fundraising: A Donor-based Approach to the Business of Raising Money (second edition)

by Ken Burnett
Published by Jossey-Bass Inc in
association with The White Lion
Press Limited. Hardback, 384 pp.
ISBN 0-7879-6089-6

Ken Burnett has completely revised and updated his classic book, *Relationship Fundraising*. Filled with illustrative case examples, donor profiles, and more than 200 action points, it is an invaluable resource for anyone concerned with effective marketing for any organisation that depends on public support to achieve its mission.

'Not since Harold Seymour's classic, *Designs for Fund Raising*, has a book of this magnitude come along.

'Ken Burnett's updated and expanded work, *Relationship Fundraising*, just may be the book to which fundraising professionals turn for the next several decades.

'It is as brilliant as it is heartfelt, as simple as it is eloquent.'
Jerry Cianciolo, *The Compleat Professional's Library*, *Contributions Magazine*, USA.

'Ken Burnett's observations, insights and practical tips for building and sustaining relationships are superb. Highly readable, this book is a solid mix of sound theory and pragmatic application.'
Kay Sprinkel Grace, author, *Beyond Fund Raising*; co-author *High Impact Philanthropy*, USA.

'This is the book that sets the agenda for fundraising communications in the twenty-first century. Engaging, inspiring, and thought-provoking, *Relationship Fundraising* is based on the unique 25-year experience of one of the world's most respected fundraisers.'
Bernard Ross, director, The Management Centre, UK; co-author, *Breakthrough Thinking for Nonprofit Organizations*.

Friends for Life: Relationship Fundraising in Practice

by Ken Burnett
Hardback, 599 pp. ISBN 0-9518971-2-8

In this accessible and entertaining sequel to *Relationship Fundraising*, Ken Burnett describes how relationship fundraising is working in a wide variety of organisations in the USA, Canada and the United Kingdom. Their stories prove that relationship fundraising really does work.

'I'm an enthusiastic fan of Ken Burnett's approach to building friends for life. His new book builds on the practical, commonsense approach to donor development he is famous for advocating.

'Great examples, an easy read – I highly recommend *Friends for Life: Relationship Fundraising in Practice*.'
Dr Judith E Nichols, CFRE, author and consultant, USA.

'*Friends for Life* is a witty, readable tour of donor-think from both sides of the Atlantic and brings together a unique collection of experiences and anecdotes from many world-class fundraisers. *Relationship Fundraising* is already a classic throughout the world and this sequel is sure to have a similar impact.'
Jennie Thompson, consultant and co-founder of Craver, Mathews, Smith and Company, USA.

'The Botton Village case history is riveting. Its lessons have a relevance beyond fundraising. This is what direct marketing should always be, but so seldom is.'
Graeme McCorkell, author and consultant, UK.

Asking Properly: The Art of Creative Fundraising

by George Smith
Hardback, 220 pp.
ISBN 0-9518971-1-X

You will never read a book quite like this. George Smith tears open the conventional wisdom of fundraising creativity and so changes the rules for an entire trade. It is irreverent, funny, savagely critical, provocative and genuinely inspiring. Above all, it is highly instructive. Read it, apply its lessons and it must enable you to raise more money.

'This book will become a classic. It's not just inspirational and a great read, there's a practical benefit on every page. When you apply George Smith's secrets you can hardly fail to improve your fundraising.'
Harvey McKinnon, president, Harvey McKinnon Associates, Canada.

'It's typically George Smith: wise, uncompromising, devastatingly critical of poor fundraising, brilliantly illustrative of what is good, full of ideas, funny, marvellously written – and exceptionally good value. In short, *Asking Properly* is one of those very few books you will keep for life.'
Pierre-Bernard Le Bas, head of fundraising, UNHCR, Switzerland.